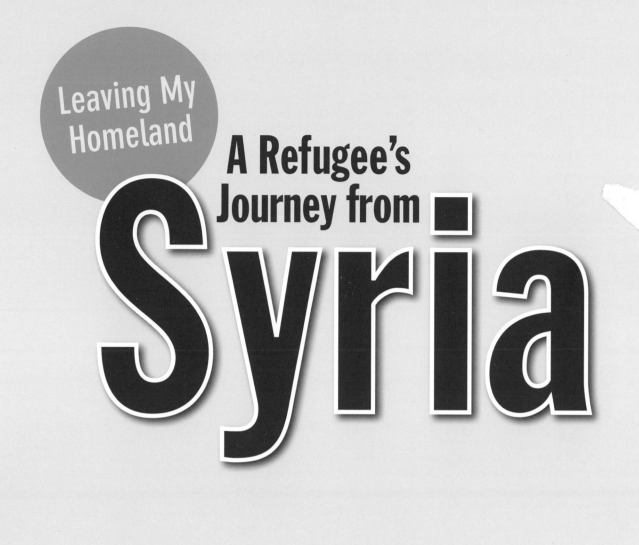

Leaving My Homeland

A Refugee's Journey from
Syria

Helen Mason

CRABTREE
Publishing Company
www.crabtreebooks.com

Crabtree Publishing Company
www.crabtreebooks.com

Author: Helen Mason

Editorial director: Kathy Middleton

Editors: Sarah Eason, Kelly Spence, and Janine Deschenes

Design: Jessica Moon

Cover design: Jessica Moon

Photo research: Rachel Blount

Proofreader: Wendy Scavuzzo

Production coordinator and prepress technician: Ken Wright

Print coordinator: Margaret Amy Salter

Consultants: Hawa Sabriye and HaEun Kim,
  Centre for Refugee Studies, York University

Publisher's Note: The story presented in this book
is a fictional account based on extensive research
of real-life accounts by refugees with the aim to reflect the
true experience of refugee children and their families.

Written and produced for Crabtree Publishing Company
by Calcium Creative

Photo Credits:
t=Top, bl=Bottom Left, br=Bottom Right

Shutterstock: Anton_Ivanov: p. 6l; Arindambanerjee: p. 29c;
ART production: pp. 5r, 8b; Artskvortsova: p. 16l; Brothers
Good: p. 7t; Istvan Csak: p. 23; Daisyx: p. 10–11b; Frank
Gaertner: p. 27t; Jazzmany: pp. 24c, 24b, 26; Kafeinkolik:
p. 15r; Anjo Kan: pp. 20, 21c; Thomas Koch: p. 15l; Ivan Kotliar:
pp. 3, 4t, 20–21b; Lawkeeper: p. 27b; Macrovector: p. 18–19b;
Mangsaab: p. 22; Svetlana Maslova: p. 13t; Mclek: p. 22–23;
Metsi: p. 6r; MSSA: pp. 18, 21t, 28t; Naeblys: p. 12c; Sarah
Nicholl: p. 8–9bg; Orlok: p. 16r; Palau: p. 12b; Procyk Radek:
p. 8t; Rkl_foto: p. 25; Seita: p. 14–15b; Eugene Sergeev:
p. 9; Jim Vallee: pp. 4b, 18–19; Ververidis Vasilis: pp. 13bl,
17; Vodograj: p. 7b; What's My Name: pp. 14–15, 25t, 29t;
Wikimedia Commons: Shamsnn: p. 10b; SMSgt George
Thompson: p. 11t; U.S. Department of State: p. 19b; Zyzzzzzy:
p. 5tl.

Cover: Shutterstock: Svetlana Maslova (right), Prazis (bottom).

Library and Archives Canada Cataloguing in Publication

Mason, Helen, 1950-, author
    A refugee's journey from Syria / Helen Mason.

(Leaving my homeland)
Includes index.
Issued in print and electronic formats.
ISBN 978-0-7787-3128-3 (hardcover).--ISBN 978-0-7787-3184-9 (softcover).--
ISBN 978-1-4271-1881-3 (HTML)

    1. Refugees--Syria--Juvenile literature. 2. Refugees--Europe--Juvenile
literature. 3. Refugee children--Syria--Juvenile literature. 4. Refugee children--
Europe--Juvenile literature. 5. Refugees--Social conditions--Juvenile literature.
6. Syria--Social conditions--Juvenile literature. 7. Boat people--Syria--Juvenile
literature. 8. Boat people--Europe--Juvenile literature. I. Title.

HV640.5.S97M37 2017   j305.9'06914095691094   C2016-907093-X
                                                    C2016-907094-8

Library of Congress Cataloging-in-Publication Data

Names: Mason, Helen, 1950- author.
Title: A refugee's journey from Syria / written by Helen Mason.
Description: New York, N.Y. : Crabtree Publishing Company, 2017. |
  Series: Leaving my homeland | Includes index.
Identifiers: LCCN 2016054844 (print) | LCCN 2016059685 (ebook) |
  ISBN 9780778731283 (reinforced library binding : alk. paper) |
  ISBN 9780778731849 (pbk. : alk. paper) |
  ISBN 9781427118813 (Electronic HTML)
Subjects: LCSH: Refugees--Syria--Juvenile literature. |
  Refugees--Europe--Juvenile literature. | Refugee children--Syria--Juvenile
  literature. | Refugee children--Europe--Juvenile literature. | Refugees--Social
  conditions--Juvenile literature. | Syria--History--Civil War, 2011---Juvenile
  literature. | Syria--Social conditions--Juvenile literature.
Classification: LCC HV640.5.S97 M37 2017 (print) | LCC HV640.5.S97 (ebook) |
  DDC 362.7/7914095691--dc23
LC record available at https://lccn.loc.gov/2016054844

Crabtree Publishing Company

www.crabtreebooks.com   1-800-387-7650

Printed in Canada/022017/CH20161214

Published in Canada
Crabtree Publishing
616 Welland Ave.
St. Catharines, ON
L2M 5V6

Published in the United States
Crabtree Publishing
PMB 59051
350 Fifth Avenue, 59th Floor
New York, New York 10118

Published in the United Kingdom
Crabtree Publishing
Maritime House
Basin Road North, Hove
BN41 1WR

Published in Australia
Crabtree Publishing
3 Charles Street
Coburg North
VIC, 3058

What Is in This Book?

Leaving Syria

A terrible **civil war** has been fought in Syria since March 2011. The war is between the Syrian government and **rebel** fighters. The rebels are fighting for **democracy**.

Syria is in the Middle East. Its neighbors are Turkey, Iraq, Jordan, Lebanon, and Israel.

EUROPE

Turkey

Mediterranean Sea

Syria

ASIA

Lebanon

Iraq

Palestine

Jordan

Israel

AFRICA

4

The conflict has destroyed towns and cities. Millions of people have lost their homes. Some Syrians who were forced from their homes remain in the country. They are **internally displaced persons (IDPs)**.

Many other Syrians have left their **homeland** since the war began. These people are **refugees**. Refugees are people who flee their homeland because of war, or other unsafe conditions. Refugees are different from **immigrants**. Immigrants chose to leave to look for better opportunities in another country. Refugees often have no choice. Since the war started, more than 4.8 million people have left Syria.

UN Rights of the Child

Every child has **rights**. Rights are privileges and freedoms that are protected by law. Refugees have the right to special protection and help. The United Nations (UN) Convention on the Rights of the Child is a document that lists the rights that all children should have. Think about these rights as you read this book.

My Homeland, Syria

Syria is an ancient land. People have lived in this area for thousands of years. Much of the country is covered in dry desert. The Euphrates River winds through Syria from north to south.

Euphrates River

Damascus

Syria's flag

Damascus is the capital of Syria.

The rich soil along the banks of the Euphrates River is good for farming. Many people have fought over the area to have access to this land. In 632 C.E., Syria was invaded by **Muslim** forces. Today, most Syrians are Muslims. They follow a religion called Islam. This faith was founded by the prophet Muhammad. The main language spoken in Syria is Arabic.

Between 1920 and 1946, Syria was under French control. The country gained **independence** from France in 1946. Syria then struggled for many years as different groups fought for power. In 1971, Hafez al-Assad became president. He helped make the country politically stable and developed strong relationships with **Western** nations, such as the United States.

But al-Assad also used his position to stay in power. He and his government made it so that Syrians were not able to vote to choose their own leader. After al-Assad's death in 2000, his son Bashar became the next president. At first, many Syrians hoped he would bring change to the country, such as allowing people to hold **protests**. But Bashar did not keep the many promises he made to the Syrian people.

A mosque is a Muslim house of worship. The Great Mosque of Damascus was built between 705 and 715 C.E.

Roj's Story: My Life Before the War

I was born in the city of Aleppo in northern Syria. I lived in an apartment with my Baba (father), mother, older brothers, and sister. My Tété (grandma) also lived with us.

Before the war, life for many children in Syria was happy. Their lives have since changed forever.

Pita is a popular bread in Syria. It is often stuffed with other foods, or eaten warm with butter.

I was only five when the war started. I do not remember a lot. But what I do remember are the good parts of life. Our apartment was above a small bakery.

Each morning, I could smell the fresh bread baking. Before and after school, my brother Ali helped dry the bread in the sun.

Our home was filled with good smells. Mama and Tété were always cooking. My sister Saja helped shape the falafel (deep-fried chickpea balls) and stir the shorba (soup). We always had plenty to eat and enough to share with others.

At school, Bakr and Abdul were my best friends. We liked to play soccer. Only we called it football because we play it with our feet.

Sometimes, Baba took us to the souk (market). He would buy us sweet squares of baklava.

Eid al-Fitr is my favorite holiday. To celebrate, we traveled to the city of Kobane to visit my Uncle Hamzah. Our family gathered at his house for a party. There was special food and fun games to play.

Syria's Story in Numbers

Before the war, almost every child in Syria went to school. Now,

2.8 million

are missing out on an education.

Baklava is a tasty dessert made from layers of pastry and chopped nuts.

The Syrian Conflict

In Syria, people do not vote for their government like they do in the United States or Canada. When people are allowed to vote for who represents them in government, it is called a democracy. Syrians knew other countries lived peacefully under democratic governments. They wanted the same opportunity to vote for their leaders.

In March 2011, a group of Syrian teenagers spray-painted a message on a wall. This was in Dar'a, a small town near the Turkish border. The message read: "The people want to topple the government!"

Syrian police put the boys in jail. This angered their families and friends. They staged a peaceful protest. Government forces attacked the protesters. Many people were killed. The next day, the army attacked people attending the funerals of those who had been killed. It then attacked the town of Dar'a.

In Damascus and many other cities, Syrians protested against the government led by Bashar al-Assad.

The Syrian people were shocked and angered. They decided to get rid of their government. Rebel groups formed to fight the government and the civil war began. The international community is now involved in the conflict, too. The Syrian government is being helped by Russia and Iran. The United States and Turkey are aiding the rebels.

The conflict is complicated by religion. Most Syrians are Muslim. Some **extremist** Muslims have formed terrorist groups. One group calls itself the **Islamic State in Iraq and the Levant** (ISIL). They believe that anyone who does not share their beliefs should be killed, including other Muslims. Many Syrians live in fear of this group.

American forces help train the Syrian rebels. They also provide aid to IDPs in parts of Syria affected by the war.

Government forces attacked Dar'a, where the protests started.

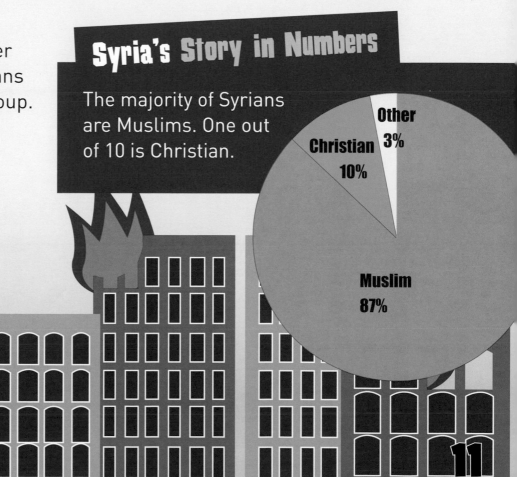

Syria's Story in Numbers

The majority of Syrians are Muslims. One out of 10 is Christian.

Other 3%

Christian 10%

Muslim 87%

Roj's Story: We Flee from Aleppo

When the war started, it was no longer safe to go out in the streets. One day, my school was bombed. Two teachers were killed. Saja, Ali, and my other brother, Mohammed, were trapped inside. Ali and Mohammed got out safely, but Saja's leg was badly hurt. She was taken to the hospital.

Aleppo is the largest city in Syria.

Kobane

Aleppo

Syria

UN Rights of the Child

You have the right to freedom and protection from war.

In many parts of Syria, it is difficult to deliver food and medicine to people in need due to the fighting.

Things got harder when Baba lost his job. He had worked as a teacher. But it was not safe to go to school anymore, so he stayed home.

Another day, Mama came home from the market upset. A bomb had exploded there. A policeman and two children were killed.

Some refugees are able to take their clothes and some household belongings with them. Others lose everything.

That night, I heard Mama and Baba talking. Two days later, we left Aleppo. Mama said I had to leave my bicycle behind.

We climbed into the back of a truck. I could hear gunfire as we drove out of the city. I fell asleep. When I woke up, we were in Kobane with Uncle Hamzah.

Nations Unite to Send Help

The United Nations (UN) is an organization made up of many countries. It was founded in 1945 after World War II. The UN works to solve problems and helps people in need.

The UN department that helps refugees is called the United Nations High Commissioner for Refugees (UNHCR). Assistance provided by the UNHCR includes emergency food and housing.

In areas with many refugees, the UNHCR and other organizations set up refugee camps. Each camp provides services to meet the needs of the refugees in the camp. These include places to sleep, grow food, and get safe water. There are also health clinics and schools.

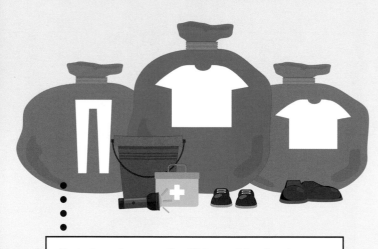

To help refugees, the UN provides basic hygiene kits. These include a bucket for carrying water, a flashlight, underwear, and band aids. Women also receive a head scarf.

Syria's Story in Numbers

In 2016, the UN gave food to
5.7 million
Syrians each month.

Many Syrians in refugee camps work to help others. Muzoon Almellehan lived in a camp in Jordan. There, she encouraged girls to continue their schooling. She now lives in England and works to raise money and awareness for Syrian refugees. She hopes to return to her homeland to help rebuild when the war ends.

In refugee camps, people temporarily live in tents or small huts.

Medical staff give needles to refugees when they arrive in camps to prevent the spread of diseases.

Roj's Story: My Life in Turkey

Uncle Hamzah had a cat named Antar. Antar is the name of a warrior who helped his people. I want to help my people some day.

We did not live in Kobane long before the fighting reached the city. It scared me. Houses were bombed. People were killed.

Airstrikes on Kobane have destroyed large parts of the town.

Baba and Uncle Hamzah took us to the Turkish border. There, they spoke to a taxi driver. He brought us to a small house. The walls were made of mud and there were only two rooms.

One morning, I looked out the door. The sky over Kobane was black with smoke. Mama said that the whole town was burning. My stomach hurt so much. Antar was in Kobane. Was he all right?

It was hard getting enough food in our new home. Baba and Mama decided to travel farther north to Suruç. There we lived in a refugee camp with thousands of other Syrians.

The camp had many rows of big white tents. It was a difficult place to live. Baba, Mama, Tété, and Uncle Hamzah spent hours lined up to receive food and clean water. Some days I felt dizzy from not having enough to eat. At night, the tent we lived in was cold.

Saja's injured leg had not improved. After a few months, she was given an artificial leg in the camp hospital. We spent hours remembering our life in Aleppo. We all wanted to go home, but it was too dangerous to return.

Children are taught in temporary schools within refugee camps.

What Paths Do Refugees Take?

Often, Syrian refugees first flee to one of the countries along the border. These countries are part of the Arab world. The people there share the same language and **customs** as many Syrians. There are millions of refugees. The countries nearby cannot afford to feed and take care of all the extra people.

Mediterranean Sea

In 2016, 115,000 Syrian refugees registered in Egypt. Many tried to reach Europe by boat.

Syria's Story in Numbers

In many camps, people receive a blanket, a bucket, a place to live, and a **ration card** when they register. This is a list of the rations a Syrian refugee might receive every week in a Jordan camp:

4.4 pounds (2 kilograms) of rice

5 pounds (2.2 kg) of flour

0.9 pounds (400 grams) of kidney beans

0.4 pounds (170 g) of lentils

0.3 pounds (125 g) of chickpeas

0.3 pounds (125 g) of canned sardines

1.25 cups (300 milliliters) of cooking oil

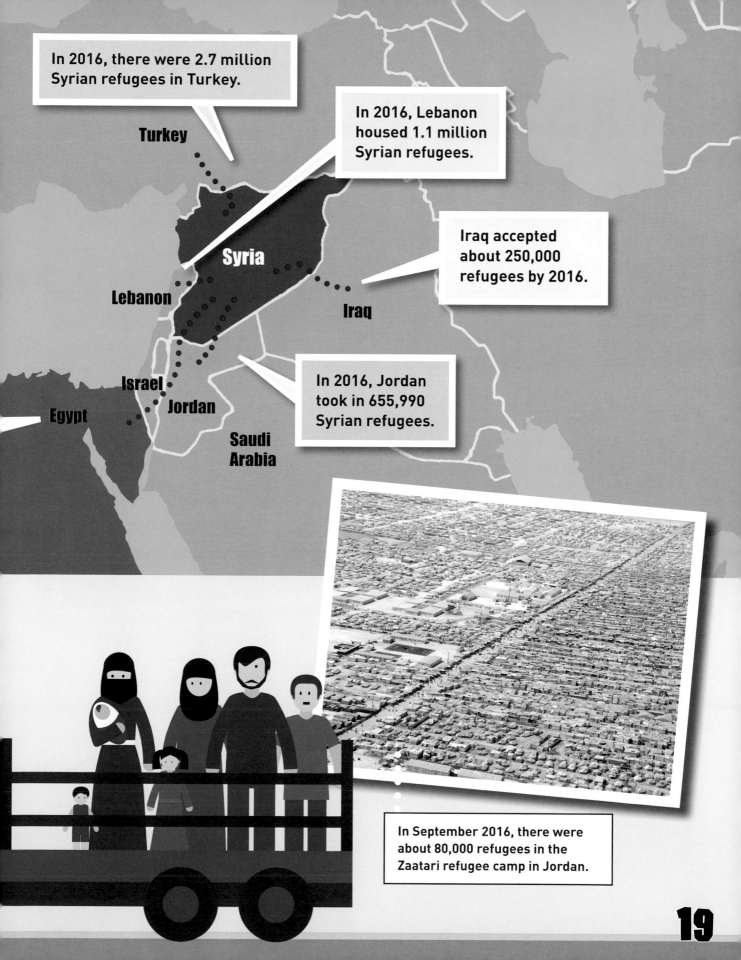

In 2016, there were 2.7 million Syrian refugees in Turkey.

In 2016, Lebanon housed 1.1 million Syrian refugees.

Iraq accepted about 250,000 refugees by 2016.

In 2016, Jordan took in 655,990 Syrian refugees.

Turkey

Syria

Lebanon

Iraq

Israel

Egypt

Jordan

Saudi Arabia

In September 2016, there were about 80,000 refugees in the Zaatari refugee camp in Jordan.

Roj's Story: We Leave for Europe

*We stayed in Suruç for many months, until my parents decided to leave. They thought we would have a better future in Europe. Baba found a **smuggler** in the camp. The smuggler said he would us get to Greece. It cost $2,000 for each of us. Tété sold all of her jewelry. With that and all our savings, we raised $12,000. That was enough for six of us.*

Uncle Hamzah and Tété decided they would stay behind. My stomach ached when I hugged them goodbye. It was dark when we left the camp. The man loaded us into a car. We drove a long way and I fell asleep. When we stopped, it was light again.

Smugglers led us onto a small boat. There were many other refugees there, too. After about an hour on the open sea, the boat's engine died. Suddenly, water started to leak into the boat. We were sinking! We tried to bail it out. But the boat continued to fill with water.

A refugee family weep for the people they lost.

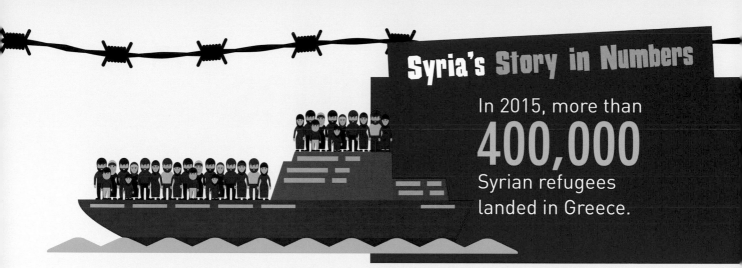

In 2015, more than

400,000

Syrian refugees landed in Greece.

Greek volunteers help to bring refugees to safety on shore.

We jumped out and started to swim. Everyone was screaming. Some people clung to barrels from the boat.

I was cold, wet, and scared when another boat arrived. Men speaking a strange language pulled me onboard. When I got to land, I found Mama, Baba, and my brothers. But we could not find Saja. She was lost.

Some Countries Welcome Refugees

Many countries around the world offer to take refugees and give them a place to live. In 2016, they agreed to accept around 208,000 Syrian refugees altogether. That is a small number compared to the need.

Some countries are afraid to accept refugees because many Syrians are Muslim. Some people associate Muslims with terrorism. They are afraid to allow Muslims into their country. This is an incorrect **stereotype**. All refugees just want a safe place to live.

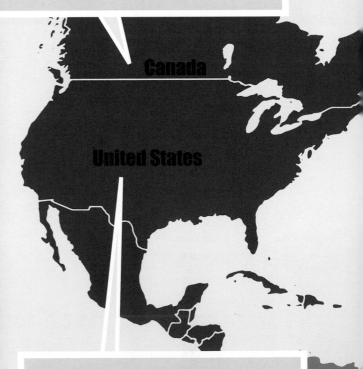

Between late 2015 and February 2016, Canada accepted 25,080 Syrian refugees. Some were sponsored, or had their journeys paid for, by the government. Others were sponsored by community groups.

Canada

United States

Anti-Muslim feeling, sometimes called Islamophobia, **is particularly strong in the United States. Muslim terrorists destroyed New York's World Trade Center in 2001. By August 2016, the country had admitted 10,000 Syrian refugees.**

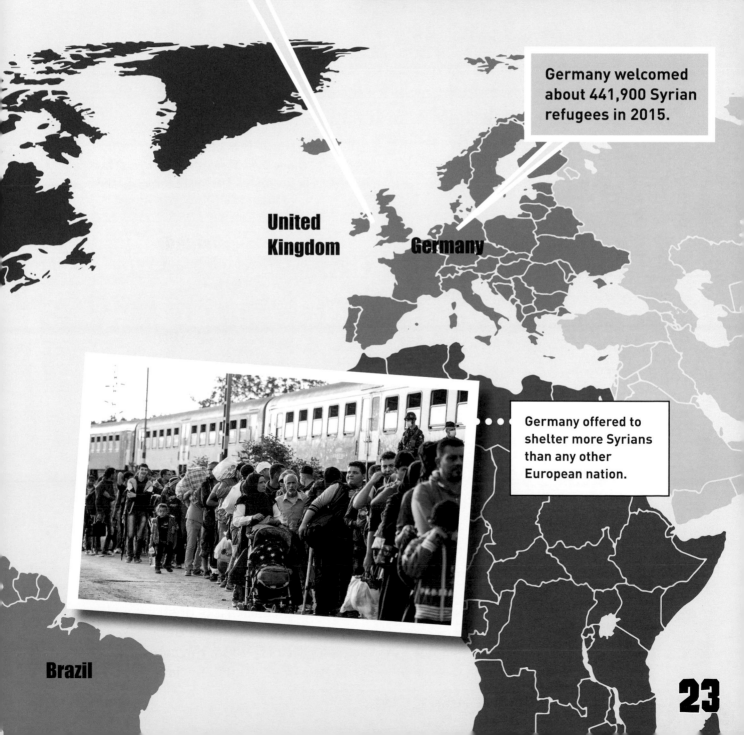

In 2015, the United Kingdom promised to host 20,000 Syrian refugees.

UN Rights of the Child

Every child has the right to be brought up in a spirit of understanding, tolerance, friendship, and peace.

Germany welcomed about 441,900 Syrian refugees in 2015.

United Kingdom

Germany

Germany offered to shelter more Syrians than any other European nation.

Brazil

Roj's Story: My New Home in Germany

*With Saja missing, we were only five. I held on tight to Baba's hand all the time we stayed in Greece. My family felt incomplete without my sister. Baba and Mama applied for **asylum** in many countries. We waited for months to hear back.*

Then, exciting news! We were granted asylum in Germany. We arrived in Germany by train. We were welcomed by a group of volunteers. They gave me warm clothes and running shoes that light up. Instead of a tent, we lived in an office building.

These Syrian refugees have just arrived in Germany. They wait for a train to take them to a refugee center.

Many people get separated on the journey to Europe. This father rejoices at finding his sons.

Syria's Story in Numbers

In 2015, more than

420,000

Syrian refugees arrived in Germany. Many came on trains from other parts of Europe.

These children play while their parents learn new skills. Play therapy can be used to help refugee children move forward after experiencing conflict.

The food was different. We got three slices of bread with butter and jam for breakfast.

Ali, Mohammed, and I started school again. I could not understand what people were saying. I had butterflies in my stomach. Then, at recess, one of my classmates smiled. He motioned for me to play ball. Soon we were playing and laughing together.

Baba and Mama are going to school. They study German. Baba hopes to get a job.

One day, we got a call. Saja is alive! She landed in a different part of Greece. Soon, we will be together.

25

Challenges Refugees Face

Finding a **host country** is the first of many challenges faced by refugees. Imagine moving to a land where you cannot speak the language or read the writing. This is what many Syrian refugees experience. Learning to speak another language is difficult. To read, a person might need to learn a whole new alphabet.

The culture in a host country can be very different. In Syria, many children live in homes with both parents and at least one grandparent. Although many women dress in Western clothing, it is common for them to wear a **hijab**.

This Syrian refugee wears Western clothes with a traditional hijab.

Many people, such as teachers, volunteer to help Syrians of all ages learn to read and write English.

For adults, finding work can be challenging. Language **barriers** and stereotypes can make it difficult to put down roots in a new place. Many refugees feel very sad about having to leave a homeland that they love. Some dream of one day returning to Syria, when it is safe. They want to return to rebuild the country. Others decide to become citizens of a new country because they believe it will offer a better future for their children. Refugees often feel pride in being part of their new country, while also feeling sad about the loss of their homeland. In many cases, refugees also have to deal with the losses of family members, or are trying to reunite their families after being separated during their journeys.

UN Rights of the Child

You have the right to practice your own culture, language, and religion—or any you choose.

You Can Help!

There are many things you can do to help refugees from places such as Syria. Learning about another culture and putting yourself in a newcomer's position is a good place to start.

 Make newcomers feel welcome. This includes smiling and saying hello. Learn to say a few words, such as hello, in Arabic. To welcome someone, say "ahlan wa sahlan."

 Share what you have learned in this book with others. Use your knowledge to write letters to local officials asking the government to support giving aid to Syrians in need.

With your class, celebrate World Refugee Day on June 20.

 Research organizations in your community that assist people affected by the Syrian civil war. Get in touch and see how you can help.

 At home, at school, and in your community, learn to work out differences of opinion with respect and patience.

Canada's welcoming
of Syrian refugees
has encouraged other
countries to do the same.

Discussion Prompts

1. Explain the difference
between a refugee, an
immigrant, and an IDP.
2. Brainstorm a list of ways you
can welcome Syrian refugees
in your community.
3. How do you think other
countries can help Syrian
refugees in need?

Glossary

asylum Protection given to refugees by a country

barriers Obstacles

civil war A war between groups of people in the same country

customs Traditional ways of doing things

democracy A form of government in which people vote for the leaders who represent them

Eid al-Fitr A Muslim holiday that marks the end of Ramadan

extremist Having a strong belief in something; often political

hijab A head covering worn by some Muslim women

homeland The country where someone was born or grew up

host country A country that offers to give refugees a home

immigrants People who leave one country to live in another

independence Having freedom from outside control

internally displaced persons (IDPs) People who are forced from their homes during a conflict but remain in their country

Islamic State in Iraq and the Levant Also called ISIL; a group of extremist Muslims who believe that people who do not share their beliefs are enemies

Islamophobia A fear or dislike of Muslims

Muslim A follower of Islam

protests Demonstrations to show disapproval of something

ration card A card that allows refugees to pick up free food

rebel A person who fights against the government of a country

refugees People who flee from their own country to another due to unsafe conditions

registered Officially recorded

rights Privileges and freedoms protected by law

smuggler A person who moves people or things illegally

stereotype An idea held about someone or something that is usually untrue

Western Refers to the countries of western Europe, North America, and Australia

Learning More

Books

Farish, Terry. *Joseph's Big Ride*. Annick Press, 2016.

Gleeson, Libby. *Mahtab's Story*. Allen and Unwin, 2008.

O'Brien, Anne Sibley. *I'm New Here*. Charlesbridge, 2015.

Ruurs, Margriet. *Stepping Stones: A Refugee Family's Journey*. Orca Book Publishers, 2016.

Websites

www.campaignlive.co.uk/article/save-children-still-shocking-second-day-dont-panic/1394164#
Watch this short video to see what could happen if you became a refugee.

www.oxfam.org.uk/education/resources/Syria
With an adult's permission, download Syrian refugee cards. Learn what is happening to Syrian refugees.

www.unicef.ca/sites/default/files/legacy/imce_uploads/images/advocacy/co/crc_poster_en.pdf
Explore the United Nations Convention on the Rights of the Child.

www.unicefusa.org/stories/syrian-childrens-courage-education-offers-hope-amid-grim-reality/30857
Read stories of Syrian children attending school in areas of conflict.

Index

About the Author

When she was growing up, Helen Mason lived in a community where many of her neighbors were refugees from Europe after World War II. She spent many hours listening to the stories of how her friends' families survived. She also learned to say hello and thank you in several different languages. This is her 33rd book.